The **Best** Advice Ever Given

Also by the Author

Teaching Riding at Summer Camp
Panorama of American Horses
Civil Rights (Vols. 1 & 2)
Get a Horse!
Take Me Home
The Second-Time Single Man's Survival Handbook
Old as the Hills
Horseback Vacation Guide
Schooling to Show
The Whole Horse Catalog
Riding's a Joy
All the King's Horses
The Beautiful Baby Naming Book
Riding for a Fall
The Polo Primer
The Ultimate Fishing Guide
Caught Me a Big 'Un
The Complete Book of the American Quarter Horse
Two Bits' Book of the American Quarter Horse
Essential Riding
The Illustrated Horseman's Dictionary
The Greatest Horse Stories Ever Told
Classic Horse Stories
1001 Smartest Things Ever Said
1001 Dumbest Things Ever Said
1001 Insults, Put-Downs, and Comebacks

The **Best** Advice Ever Given

Edited and with
an Introduction by
Steven D. Price

THE LYONS PRESS
Guilford, Connecticut
An imprint of Globe Pequot Press

To buy books in quantity for corporate use
or incentives, call **(800) 962–0973**
or e-mail **premiums@GlobePequot.com.**

The Lyons Press is an imprint of The Globe Pequot Press.

10 9 8 7 6 5

Printed in the United States of America

Designed by Sheryl P. Kober

ISBN-13: 978-1-59921-084-1

Library of Congress Cataloging-in-Publication Data is available on file.

Contents

Introduction vii

Chapter 1: Let Others Light Their Candles: Advice on a Proper Education 1

Chapter 2: Quit When the Gorilla is Tired: Advice on Life and Living 13

Chapter 3: Anvil or Hammer: Advice on Work and Leadership 55

Chapter 4: Love What You Are Doing: Advice on Success—and the Money that Sometimes Comes with It 87

Chapter 5: Bait with Your Heart: Advice on Friendship, Love, Marriage, and Other Such Mysteries . 109

Chapter 6: Throw Your Dreams: Advice to Inspire and Encourage 147

Chapter 7: Hit the Right Keys: Advice on Creativity and the Arts 179

Chapter 8: Imitate a Champion: Advice on Sports and Competition **195**

Chapter 9: A Word to the Wise: Proverbs and Other Folk Sayings **211**

Chapter 10: Enjoy Your Ice Cream: Advice on Advice **241**

Selected Quoted Sources **251**

Introduction

Advice? Who needs it?

Apparently everyone, because we're bombarded with it throughout our lives. The deluge begins with such dire parental warnings as "If you don't wear your galoshes, you'll catch your death of cold!" and "Be careful or you'll poke your eye out!" *Aesop's Fables* and cautionary fairy tales introduce us to countless other moral messages. Whatever one's faith, religious education focuses on some form of the "Do unto others" Golden Rule. High school and college literature courses include Polonius's time-worn "to thine own self be true" catalog of counsel in *Hamlet*, and *David Copperfield*'s Mr. Micawber and his classic "Annual income twenty pounds . . ." explanation of financial planning. And just when we thought we were finished with faculty advisors and guidance counselors, graduation speakers send us on our way with their advice for getting ahead.

Opinions are everywhere. Got a medical problem? Doctors will dispense advice along with pills. A legal problem? Lawyers are in the business of providing counsel, which is why they're referred to as counselors. Newspaper columnists such as "Dear Abby" and "Miss Manners" include advice in print. Religious leaders, infomercials, and television hosts like Oprah and Dr. Phil do so over the airwaves. Along with every other sort of information, the Internet is advice-rich in all manner of subjects. And throughout our lives, friends and relatives share wisdom and experience of varying degrees of usefulness that begin with a knowing nod and an "I'm going to give you a piece of advice . . . "

How we accept advice depends on what it is and by whom and how it's given. Much of the time we brush it off, because as a New England proverb suggests, "Advice would always be more acceptable if it didn't conflict with our plans." Or we run in the other direction—as the actress Marie Dressler (older readers will remember her as "Tugboat Annie") snapped, "No vice is so bad as advice." Confusing the situation is the abundance of contradictory advice, of the absence-makes-the-heart-grow-fonder variety versus "Out of sight, out of mind."

On the other hand, sound advice is not only tolerable, it's welcome. First of all, it tends to be terse—a volume of wisdom in a sentence or two—which is both appealing and expected in this sound-byte age. More important, it sets our feet on the right path; who indeed would want to disregard the global positioning that moral or practical compasses can give?

That's what you'll find in this book. Included is advice on education ("Formal education will make you a living. Self-education will make you a fortune."—Jim Rohn), life and living ("Don't carry a grudge. While you're carrying the grudge, the other guy's out dancing."—Buddy Hackett), and success of a personal and financial nature ("You can have it all. You just can't have it all at one time."—Oprah Winfrey).

Also represented here are both romantic and platonic love and friendship ("Immature love says: 'I love you because I need you.' Mature love says: 'I need you because I love you.'"—Erich Fromm), inspiration ("If you can dream it, you can do it."—Walt Disney), and creativity and the arts ("Take the best that exists and make it better. If it doesn't exist, create it."—Sir Henry Royce).

Sports and competition weigh in ("One hundred percent of shots not taken don't go in."—Wayne Gretzky), as do business and leadership ("If two men on the same job agree all the time, then one is unnecessary. If they disagree all the time, then both are useless."—Darryl Zanuck), and proverbs and folk sayings ("If you chase two rabbits, both will escape."—Spanish saying). And if you're not wise enough by then, the book concludes with—of all things—advice about advice ("Don't take a butcher's advice on how to cook meat. If he knew, he'd be a chef."—Andy Rooney).

Readers of my earlier compilations have asked which quotations were my favorites. In the event the same question occurs to you here, my answer remains the same: it depends. When I'm in good spirits or feeling sentimental, any of the warm, fuzzy quotations resonate, such as the bit of cowboy wisdom that points out, "The best sermons are lived, not preached." But if I'm in a dour mood, especially after watching the nightly news' cataclysmic chronicles of human folly and disaster, Damon Runyon's observation that "All life is six to five against" makes an eminently good way to view the world.

Another question I've been asked is, "Are these really the best? Aren't there others?" Here the answer can be more definite: I think so, and yes. The quotations you'll find in this book cover all aspects of human existence, including life itself. Certainly there are others, and many have indeed been perceptively expressed or elegantly phrased, but whatever their subjects might be, you'll find them covered in these pages. (I also excluded commandments and orders, which are distinguished from advice by their implied or expressed threat of punishment if disobeyed.)

Many people contributed their favorite quotations and sources in the course of this compilation's creation, for who can refuse the request to "tell me some good advice"? Although there are far too many people to acknowledge individually, there is one person whom I want to publicly thank, which I'll do in the form of advice: Don't even think about writing or compiling a book unless you can work with as capable and encouraging an editor as Holly Rubino.

Steven D. Price
New York, New York
January 2006

Chapter One

Let Others Light Their Candles

{Advice on a Proper Education}

If you have **knowledge**, let others **light their** candles in it.

—Margaret Fuller

"Try to learn something about everything and everything about something."

—Thomas Henry Huxley

In youth we **learn**; in age we **understand**.

—Marie von Ebner-Eschenbach

Learn as though you would
never be able to master it;
hold it as though you would
be in fear of losing it.

—Confucius

Education is only the ladder with
which to gather fruit from the tree of
knowledge, not the fruit itself.

—Anonymous

Those who cannot learn from
history are doomed to repeat it.

—George Santayana

Never seem wiser, nor more learned,
than the people you are with. **Wear
your learning, like your watch,
in a private** pocket, and do not merely
pull it out and strike it merely to show
that you have one.

—Lord Chesterfield

"It's important to watch
what you put in your mind."

—Linda Knight

Study as if you were going to **live forever;**
live as if you were going to **die tomorrow.**

—Maria Mitchell

Never help a child with a task at which he feels he can succeed.

—Maria Montessori

The man who does not read **good books** has no advantage over the man who cannot **read them.**

—Mark Twain

"We cannot hold a torch to light another's path without brightening our own."

—Ben Sweetland

Trust should be the basis for all our **moral** training.

—Sir Robert Baden-Powell

"To bring up a child in the way he should go, travel that way yourself once in a while."

—Josh Billings

Parents must get across the idea that "**I love you always,** but sometimes I do not love your behavior."

—Amy Vanderbilt

Acquire new knowledge whilst thinking over the old, and you may **become a teacher of others.**

—Confucius

Correction does much, but encouragement does more. Encouragement after censure is as the sun after a shower.

—Johann von Goethe

The **proof** that you know something is that you are able to **teach it.**

—Aristotle

"If you want to know the taste of a pear, you must change the pear by eating it yourself. If you want to know the theory and methods of revolution, you must take part in revolution. All genuine knowledge originates in direct experience."

—Mao Tse-tung

Give a man a fish, and you have **fed him for a day.** Teach a man to fish, and you have fed him for the **rest of his life.**

—Chinese proverb

Give a man a fish and he has food for a day; teach him how to fish and you can get rid of him for the entire weekend.

—Anonymous

The wise learn many things from their enemies.

—Aristophanes

It's so simple to be wise. Just think of something stupid to say and then don't say it.

—Sam Levenson

"You can tell whether a man is clever by his answers. You can tell whether a man is wise by his questions."

—Naguib Mahfouz

Doubt everything at least once, even the proposition that two times two equals four.

—Georg C. Lichtenberg

A foolish consistency is the hobgoblin of little minds.

—Ralph Waldo Emerson

Nothing is **more important** for the public welfare than to form and train our youth in **wisdom and virtue**.

—Benjamin Franklin

Never look down on anyone unless you're helping him up.

—Jesse Jackson

The only **real mistake** is the one from which we l**earn nothing**.

—John Powell

Formal education will make you **a living.**
Self-education will make you **a fortune.**

—Jim Rohn

Learn all you can about people in other parts of the world. Understanding how people in other countries live and work and play teaches us to respect them and **promotes peace everywhere.**

—Carol Bellamy

Real education should educate us out of self into something far finer; into a selflessness which links us with all humanity.

—Nancy Astor

Chapter Two

Quit When the Gorilla Is Tired

{Advice on Life and Living}

[Life] is a little like **wrestling a gorilla.**
You don't quit when you're tired—you
quit when the gorilla is tired.

—Robert Strauss

You can get much further with a
kind word and a gun than you can
with a kind word alone.

—Al Capone

Don't hurry. Don't worry. You're only
here for a short visit. So **don't forget
to stop and smell the roses.**

—Walter Hagen

Never go to a doctor whose office plants have **died**.

—Erma Bombeck

"Saying 'Gesundheit!' doesn't really help the common cold, but it's every bit as effective as anything the medical profession has prescribed."

—Anonymous

Be careful about reading health books. You may die of a **misprint**.

—Mark Twain

"Yesterday is a canceled check; tomorrow is a promissory note; today is the only cash you have, so spend it wisely."

—Kay Lyons

Happy the man, and happy he alone, He who can call today his own; He who, secure within, can say, "Tomorrow do thy worst, for **I have lived today.**"

—Horace,

as translated by John Dryden

Health is the greatest gift, contentment the greatest wealth, faithfulness the best relationship.

—Buddha

In baiting a mousetrap with cheese, be sure to leave room for the mouse.

—H. H. Munro (Saki)

There is one piece of advice, in a life of study, which I think no one will object to; and that is, every now and then to be completely idle—to do nothing at all.

—Sydney Smith

"The time to relax is when you don't have time for it."

—Sydney J. Harris

The only way to get rid of a temptation is to yield to it.

—Oscar Wilde

Don't worry about **avoiding temptation** . . . as you grow older, it will **avoid you.**

—Winston Churchill

There's only one corner of the universe
you can be certain of improving, and
that's your own self.

—Aldous Huxley

Have no fear of perfection—you'll
never reach it.

—Salvador Dali

"Never lend your car
to anyone to whom
you have given birth."

—Erma Bombeck

Life is an echo—what you send out
  comes back.

—Anonymous

The wise man will always
  reflect concerning the quality,
  not the quantity, of life.

—Lucius Annaeus Seneca

Do not try to live forever.
  You will **not succeed.**

—George Bernard Shaw

"If you're going to do something tonight that you'll be
sorry for tomorrow morning,
sleep late."

—Henny Youngman

Don't eat yellow snow.

—Anonymous

Don't carry a grudge. While you're carrying
the grudge, the other guy's out dancing.

—Buddy Hackett

Life is change. Growth is optional.
Choose wisely.

—Karen Kaiser Clark

When you **come to a fork** in the road,
take it.

—Yogi Berra

"A man has to live with
himself, and he should see
to it that he always has
good company."

—Charles Evans Hughes

He who has health **has hope.** And he who
has hope **has everything.**

—Arabian proverb

He that finds discontentment
in one place is not likely to find
happiness in another.

—Aesop, *The Ass and His Masters*

What's a **man's first duty?** The answer's
brief: **to be himself.**

—Henrik Ibsen

What the hell—you might be right, you might be wrong . . . **but don't just avoid.**

—Katharine Hepburn

The attributes of a great lady may still be found in the rule of the four S's: Sincerity, Simplicity, Sympathy, and Serenity.

—Emily Post

It is dangerous to be **sincere** unless you are **also stupid.**

—George Bernard Shaw

"In matters of grave importance, style, not sincerity, is the vital thing."

—Oscar Wilde

Love yourself, respect yourself. Never sell yourself short. **Believe in yourself** regardless of what people think. You can accomplish anything, absolutely anything, if you **set your mind to it.**

—Marcus Allen

A good time for laughing is when you can.

—Jessamyn West

Do not take life too seriously. You will never get out of it alive.

—Elbert Hubbard

"Subdue your appetites, my dears, and you've conquered human nature."

—Dorothy Canfield Fisher

A man should never be ashamed to admit he has been in the wrong, which is but saying, in other words, that he is wiser today than he was yesterday.

—Alexander Pope

In the **fight** between **you** and the world,
back the world.

—Franz Kafka

Expecting the world to treat you
fairly because you are good is like
expecting the bull not to charge
because you are a vegetarian.

—Dennis Wholey

Always **acknowledge a fault** frankly.
This will throw those in authority off their
guard and give you **opportunity** to
commit more.

—Mark Twain

If you're going to **kick authority** in the
teeth, you might as well **use two feet.**

—Keith Richards

Always do sober what you said
you'd do drunk. That will teach
you to keep your mouth shut.

—Ernest Hemingway

Don't worry about the world **coming
to an end** today. It's already tomorrow
in Australia.

—Charles Schulz

"The etiquette advice you need is how to say no politely. You do it cheerfully, with apologies but no excuses. 'I'm so sorry, I can't this time; I hope you find someone' is all that is necessary."

—Judith Martin (Miss Manners)

It is **not what we do**, but also what **we do not do**, for which **we are** accountable.

—Jean-Baptiste Molière

"Teach thy tongue to say
'I do not know,' and thou
shalt progress."

—Moses Maimonides

Knowing is not **enough;** we must apply.
Willing is not enough; **we must do.**

—Johann von Goethe

You never know what is enough
unless you know what is more
than enough.

—William Blake

From what we get, we can make a living; what we give, however, makes a life.

—Arthur Ashe

Start by doing what is necessary; then do what is possible; and suddenly you are doing the impossible.

—St. Francis of Assisi

You can't do anything about the length of your life, but you can do something about its width and depth.

—H. L. Mencken

"A young man who desires to know all that in all ages in all lands has been thought by the best minds, and wishes to make a synthesis of all these thoughts for the future benefit of mankind, is laying up for himself a very miserable old age."

—Max Beerbohm

Don't go around saying the **world owes you a living.** The world owes you nothing. **It was here first.**

—Mark Twain

You've got to be **very careful** if you don't know where you are going, because you **might not get there.**

—Yogi Berra

Nature gives you the face you have at twenty; it is up to you to merit the face you have at fifty.

—Coco Chanel

Neither should a ship rely on one small anchor, nor should life rest on a **single hope.**

—Epictetus

When people talk, listen completely.
Most people never listen.

—Ernest Hemingway

A day without laughter is a day wasted.

—Charlie Chaplin

"Be thankful for what you
have; you'll end up having
more. If you concentrate
on what you don't have,
you will never, ever have
enough."

—Oprah Winfrey

You must try to generate **happiness** within **yourself.** If you aren't happy in one place, chances are you won't be **happy** anyplace.

—Ernie Banks

It's a funny thing about life: If you refuse to accept anything but the very best, you will very often get it.

—W. Somerset Maugham

You have to find it. **No one else** can find it for you.

—Bjorn Borg

"Remember, no one can make you feel inferior without your consent."

—Eleanor Roosevelt

If thine enemy offend thee, give his child a drum.

—Chinese curse

Always forgive your enemies; nothing annoys them so much.

—Oscar Wilde

When the water reaches the upper level, follow the rats.

—Claude Swanson

It is better to die on **your feet** than to live on **your knees.**

—Emiliano Zapata

"Death is not the greatest loss in life. The greatest loss is what dies inside us while we live."

—Norman Cousins

Dying is a very dull, dreary affair.
And my advice to you is to have
nothing whatever to do with it.

—W. Somerset Maugham

That you may retain your **self-respect,**
it is better to displease the people by doing
what you know is **right,** than to temporar-
ily please them by doing what you know is
wrong.

—William J. H. Boetcker

I must **respect the opinions** of others
even if I disagree with them.

—Herbert H. Lehman

"Good character is contagious; pass it on to others."

—Anonymous

It's **lack of faith** that makes people afraid of meeting challenges, and **I believed** in myself.

—Muhammad Ali

"Play the hand you're dealt."

—Anonymous

"Don't look back. Something might be gaining on you."

—Satchel Paige

If you do not tell the **truth** about yourself you cannot **tell it** about other people.

—Virginia Woolf

Don't waste your time thinking about who you ought to be; just be content with who you're becoming.

—Anonymous

Be pleasant until ten o'clock in
the morning and the rest of the
day will take care of itself.

—Elbert Hubbard

Think in the morning. **Act** in the noon.
Eat in the evening. **Sleep** in the night.

—William Blake

"The first recipe for
happiness is: Avoid
too lengthy meditation
on the past."

—André Maurois

You can **only milk a cow** so long,
and then you're left **holding the pail.**

—Hank Aaron

It does no good to think
moralistically about how much
time we waste. Wasted time is
usually good soul time.

—Thomas Moore

Never let your **sense of morals** get
in the way of **doing what's right.**

—Isaac Asimov

"Nothing ruins the truth like stretching it."

—Anonymous

Flattery won't **hurt you** if you don't **swallow it.**

—Kin (Frank McKinney) Hubbard

"If you have enough butter, anything is good."

—Julia Child

"Life is uncertain.
Eat dessert first."

—Ernestine Ulmer

One of these days in your travels,
a guy is going to come up to you and
show you a nice brand-new deck of cards
on which the seal is not yet broken,
and this guy is going to offer to bet
you that he can make the Jack of Spades
jump out of the deck and squirt cider in
your ear. But, son, **do not bet this
man,** for as sure as you are standing
there, you are going to end up with an
earful of cider.

—Damon Runyon

Dress simply. If you wear a dinner jacket, don't wear anything else on it . . . like lunch or dinner.

—George Burns

Start every day off with a smile and get it over with.

—W. C. Fields

"You've got to take the bitter with the sour."

—Samuel Goldwyn

Never purchase beauty products in a **hardware** store.

—Miss Piggy

"The secret to staying young is to live honestly, eat slowly, and lie about your age."

—Lucille Ball

The **greatest thing** in the world is to know how to **belong to oneself.**

—Michel de Montaigne

Age is whatever you think it is.
You are as old as you think
you are.

—Muhammad Ali

Stewart [Brand] and his team put out
several issues of the *Whole Earth Catalog*,
and then when it had run its course,
they put out a final issue. . . . On the back
cover of their final issue was a photograph
of an early morning country road, the kind
you might find yourself hitchhiking on if you
were so adventurous. Beneath were the
words, "Stay hungry, stay foolish."
It was their farewell message as they
signed off. "Stay hungry, stay foolish."

—Steve Jobs

If you're going to be able to **look back** on something and laugh about it, you might as well **laugh about it now.**

—Marie Osmond

"There are two things to aim for in life: first, to get when you want; and, after that, to enjoy it. Only the wisest of mankind achieve the second."

—Logan Pearsall Smith

Life is an adventure in **forgiveness.**

—Norman Cousins

Do whatever comes your way to do as well as you can. Think as little as possible about yourself. Think as much as possible about other people. Dwell on things that are interesting. Since you get more joy out of giving joy to others, you should put a good deal of thought into the happiness that you are able to give.

—Eleanor Roosevelt

Anyone who has never made a mistake has never tried anything new.

—Albert Einstein

It is better to ask some of
the questions than to know
all the answers.

—James Thurber

You must live for what you believe
in and believe in what you live for.

—Anonymous

The easiest person to deceive
is one's own self.

—Edward Bulwer-Lytton

"The unvarnished truth
is always better than the
best-dressed lie."

—Ann Landers

If there was **nothing** wrong in the world,
there wouldn't be **anything** for us to do.

—George Bernard Shaw

The strongest possible piece of
advice I would give to any young
woman is: Don't screw around,
and don't smoke.

—Edwina Currie

If a **dog** will not come to you after having
looked you in the **face**, you should go home
and **examine** your conscience.

—Woodrow Wilson

All human beings should try to
learn before they die what they
are running from, and to, and why.

—James Thurber

I came to the conclusion long ago that
all life is **six to five against.**

—Damon Runyon

"In three words I can sum up everything I've learned about life: It goes on."

—Robert Frost

This above all: to thine own self be true, And it must follow, as the night the day, Thou canst not then be false to any man.

—Polonius, from *Hamlet*, William Shakespeare

Chapter Three

Anvil or Hammer

{Advice on Work and Leadership}

In this **world** a man must either be **anvil** or **hammer**.

—Henry Wadsworth Longfellow

"The beginning is the most important part of the work."

—Plato

No labor, however humble, is **dishonoring.**

—The Talmud

The secret of joy in work is contained in one word: excellence. To know how to do something well is to enjoy it.

—Pearl Buck

"The secret of getting ahead is getting started. The secret of getting started is breaking your complex overwhelming tasks into small manage-able tasks, and then starting on the first one."

—Mark Twain

To kill time is not murder,
  it's suicide.

—William James

The less one has to do, the less time one
  finds to do it in.

—Lord Chesterfield

"Vision without action is a
daydream. Action without
vision is a nightmare."

—Japanese proverb

If you are **planning** for one year, grow rice. If you are planning for twenty years, grow trees. If you are planning for centuries, **grow men.**

—Chinese proverb

"You don't manage people, you manage things. You lead people."

—Grace Hopper

Give me a stock clerk **with a goal** and I'll give you a man who will make history. Give me a man **with no goals** and I'll give you a stock clerk.

—J. C. Penney

Expect **problems** and eat them for
breakfast.

—Alfred A. Montapert

"Creating without claiming,
Doing without taking credit,
Guiding without interfering,
This is Primal Virtue."

—Lao-tzu

We can't **solve problems** by using the
same kind of thinking we used when we
created them.

—Albert Einstein

You can't turn back the clock.
But you can wind it up again.

—Bonnie Prudden

Know each other as if you were **brothers**;
negotiate deals as if you were **strangers**
to **each other.**

—Arabian proverb

Pull the string, and it will follow
wherever you wish. Push it, and
it will go nowhere at all.

—Dwight D. Eisenhower

If you can't **convince** them, **confuse**
them.

—Harry S. Truman

"Don't get mad. Don't
get even. Just get elected,
then get even."

—James Carville

If you do what you've **always done,**
you'll get what you've **always gotten.**

—Anthony Robbins

"No one ever ever won a chess game by betting on each move. Sometimes you have to move backward to get a step forward."

—Amar Gopal Bose

Take rest; a field that has rested gives a **bountiful crop.**

—Ovid

Measure twice, cut once.

—Craftsman's adage

"Forgive your enemies,
but never forget their
names."

—John F. Kennedy

Don't ever **take a fence down** until you
know **why it was put up.**

—Robert Frost

Don't agonize. Organize.

—Florynce Kennedy

Stop stewing and **start** doing!

—Denis Waitley

Work as if you were to **live a hundred years.** Pray as if you were to **die tomorrow.**

—Benjamin Franklin

"If you're not failing every now and again, it's a sign you're not doing anything very innovative."

—Woody Allen

I am not discouraged, because
   every wrong attempt discarded
   is another step forward.
                         —Thomas Edison

"When I go fishing,
   I don't bait the hook with
   something *I* like to eat."
                         —Will Rogers

You don't lead by hitting people
   over the head—that's assault,
   not leadership.
                         —Dwight D. Eisenhower

"No one can give you authority. But if you act like you have it, others will believe you do."

—Karen Ireland

There are no office hours for leaders.

—James Cardinal Gibbons

"Change before you have to."

—Jack Welch

"The way to do research is to attack the facts at the point of greatest astonishment."

—Celia Green

If two men on the same job **agree** all the time, then one is unnecessary. If they disagree all the time, then both **are useless.**

—Darryl Zanuck

Presence is more than just being there.

—Malcolm Forbes

The best way to **escape** from a problem
is to **solve it.**

—Alan Saporta

You are your work. Don't trade the
stuff of your life, time, for nothing more
than dollars. That's a **rotten bargain.**

—Rita Mae Brown

You can either take action,
or you can hang back and hope
for a miracle. Miracles are great,
but they are so unpredictable.

—Peter F. Drucker

"When a thing is done,
it's done. Don't look back.
Look forward to your
next objective."

—George C. Marshall

The secret of business is to know
something nobody else knows.

—Aristotle Onassis

As long as you're going to be thinking
anyway, **think big.**

—Donald Trump

I once **complained** to my father that
I didn't seem to be able to do things the
same way other people did. Dad's
advice? "Margo, don't be a sheep.
People hate sheep. **They eat sheep.**"

—Margo Kaufman

"The best executive is the
one who has sense enough
to pick good men to do what
he wants done, and self-
restraint enough to keep
from meddling with them
while they do it."

—Theodore Roosevelt

"A constructive, useful life, good works, and good relationships are as valid as writing poetry or inventing a machine. Anything that one does well and obtains satisfaction from is a good enough reason for living. To be a decent human being that people like and feel better for knowing is enough."

—Robert Gould

Never ascribe to malice that
which can adequately be explained
by incompetence.

—Napoleon Bonaparte

You have to learn to treat people
as a resource. . . . You have to
ask not what do they cost, but
what is the yield, what can
they produce?

—Peter F. Drucker

Experience **taught me** a few things.
One is to **listen** to your gut, no matter
how good something sounds on paper.
The second is that you're generally
better off sticking with **what you
know**. And the third is that sometimes
your best investments are the **ones
you don't make.**

—Donald Trump

Be nice to people on your way up
because you'll meet them on your
way down.

—Wilson Mizner

Big doesn't necessarily mean better. Sunflowers aren't better than violets.

—Edna Ferber

Often you just have to rely on **your** intuition.

—Bill Gates

"Security isn't what the wise person looks for; it's opportunity."

—Earl Nightingale

It's not so much how busy you are, but why you are busy. The bee is praised. The mosquito is swatted.

—Mary O'Connor

"Everyone is a genius at least once a year; a real genius has his original ideas closer together."

—Georg C. Lichtenberg

Take your work seriously, but never yourself.

—Margot Fonteyn

Don't look at the problem.
The more you look at problems,
the more problems will come.
Look for the solution.

—Lisa Pragnelle

Don't find **fault**. Find a **remedy**.

—Henry Ford

You have to **learn the rules**
of the game—and then you have
to **play better** than anyone else.

—Dianne Feinstein

Those who say it can't be done
are usually interrupted by others
doing it.

—James A. Baldwin

To fulfill a **dream**, to be allowed to sweat
over lonely labor, to be given a chance to
create, is the meat and potatoes of life.
The money is **the gravy.**

—Bette Davis

If you don't have time to do
it right, you must have time
to do it over.

—Anonymous

Take calculated **risks**. That is
quite different from **being rash**.

—George S. Patton

"Get action. Do things;
be sane, don't fritter away
your time; create, act, take
a place wherever you are
and be somebody; get
action. Seize the moment.
Man was never intended
to become an oyster."

—Theodore Roosevelt

Quigley's Law: Whoever has any authority over you, no matter how small, will attempt to use it.

—Anonymous

"If you wish to know what a man is, place him in authority."

—Yugoslav proverb

No pressure, no diamonds.

—Mary Case

Do not confuse motion and
progress. A rocking horse
keeps moving but does not
make any progress.

—Alfred A. Montapert

Life without industry is guilt,
and industry without art is brutality.

—John Ruskin

You can't build a reputation
on what you intend to do.

—Liz Smith

Work smarter, not harder—
laziness is the mother of invention.

—Regina Reynolds

"You never get a second
chance to make a first
impression."

—Anonymous

In short, the way to wealth, if you desire it,
is as plain as the way to market. It depends
chiefly on two words, industry and frugality;
that is, waste neither time nor money,
but make the best use of both.

—Benjamin Franklin

The secret of getting ahead is getting started.

—Sally Berger

Don't worry about people **stealing** your ideas. If your ideas are **any good**, you'll have to ram them down people's throats.

—Howard Aiken

Excellence in any department can be attained only by the labor of a lifetime; it is not to be purchased at a lesser price.

—Samuel Johnson

If you want **creative workers,**
give them enough **time to play.**

—John Cleese

If you break 100, watch your
golf. If you break 80, watch your
business.

—Joey Adams

Everyone has an **invisible** sign hanging
from their neck saying, "Make me feel
important." **Never forget** this message
when working with **people.**

—Mary Kay Ash

"Never say no when a client asks for something, even if it is the moon. You can always try, and anyhow, there is plenty of time afterwards to explain that it was not possible."

—Richard M. Nixon

It's all to do with the training. You can do a lot if you're properly trained.

—Queen Elizabeth II

"My grandfather once told me that there were two kinds of people: those who do the work and those who take the credit. He told me to try to be in the first group. There was much less competition."

—Indira Gandhi

Chapter Four

Love What You Are Doing

{Advice on Success—and the Money
that Sometimes Comes with It}

Success is not the **key to happiness.**
Happiness is the key to success. **If you
love** what you are doing, you will **be
successful.**

—Albert Schweitzer

Love what you do. Get good at it.
Competence is a rare commodity
in this day and age. And let the
chips fall where they may.

—Jon Stewart

You can have it all. You just can't
have it all **at one time.**

—Oprah Winfrey

"A true measure of your worth includes all the benefits others have gained from your success."

—Cullen Hightower

A strong, positive **self-image** is the best possible preparation for **success**.

—Dr. Joyce Brothers

Keep away from people who try to **belittle your ambitions.** Small people always do that, but the really great make you feel that you, too, **can become great.**

—Mark Twain

Instead of thinking about **where you are,** think about where you want to be. It takes twenty years of hard work to become an **overnight success.**

—Diana Rankin

"If one advances confidently in the direction of one's dreams, and endeavors to live the life which one has imagined, one will meet with a success unexpected in common hours."

—Henry David Thoreau

Don't aim for success if you want it; just do what you love and believe in, and it will come naturally.

—David Frost

Look at the real successes, the people who make a lot more money than you—Elton John, Captain Kangaroo, anybody from Saudi Arabia, Big Bird, and so on. They all dress funny—and they all succeed. Are you catching on?

—Dave Barry

Part of the secret of a success in life is to eat what you like and let the food fight it out inside.

—Mark Twain

Formula for success: **Underpromise** and **overdeliver.**

—Tom Peters

"The test of a successful person is not an ability to eliminate all problems before they arise, but to meet and work out difficulties when they do arise. We must be willing to make an intelligent compromise with perfection lest we wait forever before taking action. It's still good advice to cross bridges as we come to them."

—David Joseph Schwartz

Successful leaders make sure that they succeed! They are **not afraid** of strength in others. Andrew Carnegie wanted to put on his gravestone, "Here lies a man who knew how to put into his service more able men than **he was himself.**"

—Peter F. Drucker

Many of life's failures are people who did not realize how close they were to success when they gave up.

—Thomas Edison

"How far you go in life depends on your being tender with the young, compassionate with the aged, sympathetic with the striving, and tolerant of the weak and strong. Because someday in your life you will have been all of these."

—George Washington Carver

Resentment is one burden that is incompatible with **your success**. Always be the first to forgive; and **forgive yourself first always.**

—Dan Zadra

Six essential qualities that are the key to success: sincerity, personal integrity, humility, courtesy, wisdom, charity.

—William Menninger

The only failure is not to try.

—George Clooney

"If at first you do succeed, try to hide your astonishment."

—Anonymous

Success and **rest** don't sleep **together**.

—Russian proverb

"The road to wisdom?
Well, it's plain and simple
to express: Err and err
and err again, but less
and less and less."

—Piet Hein

"He has achieved success who has lived well, laughed often, and loved much; who has enjoyed the trust of pure women, the respect of intelligent men, and the love of little children; who has filled his niche and accomplished his task; who has left the world better than he found it, whether by an improved poppy, a perfect poem, or a rescued soul; who has never lacked appreciation of Earth's beauty or failed

to express it; who has
always looked for the best
in others and given them
the best he had; whose life
was an inspiration; whose
memory a benediction."

—Betty Anderson Stanley

(often attributed in a

somewhat different form to

Ralph Waldo Emerson)

Here's what would be pitiful . . .
if your income grew and you didn't.

—Jim Rohn

With **money** in your pocket, you are wise and you are handsome and you **sing well too.**

—Yiddish proverb

"People who work sitting down get paid more than people who work standing up."

—Ogden Nash

Dishonest money **dwindles away,** but he who gathers money little by little **makes it grow.**

—Proverbs 13:11

Remember that money is of the prolific, generating nature. Money can beget money, and its offspring can beget more, and so on.

—Benjamin Franklin

Try not to become a man of **success**, but rather try to become a man of **value**.

—Albert Einstein

"Money often costs too much."

—Ralph Waldo Emerson

For the love of money is the root of all evil: which while some coveted after, they have erred from the faith, and pierced themselves through with many sorrows.

—Timothy 6:10

You cannot **motivate** the best people with money. Money is just a way to keep score. The best people in any field are motivated by **passion**.

—Eric S. Raymond

If you want to know what a man is really like, notice how he acts when he loses money.

—Spanish proverb

"Never work just for money or for power. They won't save your soul or help you sleep at night."

—Marian Wright Edelman

There are no pockets in a shroud.

—Anonymous

Beware of little expenses. A small leak will sink a great ship.

—Benjamin Franklin

"It's good to have money and the things that money can buy, but it's good, too, to make sure you haven't lost the things that money can't buy."

—George Horace Lorimer

Annual income twenty pounds, annual expenditure nineteen six, **result happiness.** Annual income twenty pounds, annual expenditure twenty pounds ought and six, **result misery.**

—Mr. Micawber, from *David Copperfield*,

Charles Dickens

Resolve not to be poor: whatever you have, spend less. Poverty is a great enemy to human happiness; it certainly destroys liberty, and it makes some virtues impracticable, and others extremely difficult.

—Samuel Johnson

Buy land. They ain't making any
more of the stuff.

—Will Rogers

It isn't necessary to be **rich and famous**
to be happy. It's only necessary to be **rich.**

—Alan Alda

"Being rich is having money;
being wealthy is having
time."

—Stephen Swid

Never spend your money before you have it.

—Thomas Jefferson

I've never been poor,
only broke. Being poor
is a frame of mind.
Being broke is only
a temporary situation.

—Mike Todd

Always borrow money from a **pessimist**.
He doesn't **expect to be paid back**.

—Anonymous

Remember this saying, "The good paymaster is lord of another man's purse." He that is known to pay punctually and exactly to the time he promises may at any time and on any occasion raise all the money his friends can spare.

—Benjamin Franklin

Where large sums of money are concerned, it is advisable to trust nobody.

—Agatha Christie

Chapter Five

Bait with Your Heart

{Advice on Friendship, Love,
Marriage, and Other Such Mysteries}

When you fish for love, bait with your heart, not your brain.

—Mark Twain

The **best proof** of love is **trust.**

—Dr. Joyce Brothers

You'll never forget your first lover, so try to make it someone you won't regret thinking about for the rest of your life.

—Dr. Ruth Westheimer

"Never play cards with a man called Doc. Never eat at a place called Mom's. Never sleep with a woman whose troubles are worse than your own."

—Nelson Algren

Do **not** walk behind me; I may not **lead**. Do **not** walk in front of me; I may not **follow**. Walk beside me, that we may **be as one**.

—Ute saying

For **marriage** to be a success, every woman and every man should have her and his **own** bathroom. **The end.**

—Catherine Zeta-Jones

"Keep your eyes wide open before marriage, half shut afterwards."

—Benjamin Franklin

As long as you know that most **men are like children,** you know everything.

—Coco Chanel

The quickest way to know
a woman is to go shopping
with her.

—Marcelene Cox

By all means, **marry.** If you get a good wife,
you'll become **happy;** if you get a bad one,
you'll become **a philosopher.**

—Socrates

Never advise anyone to go to war
or to marry.

—Spanish proverb

In buying a **horse** and taking a **wife**, shut your eyes and commend yourself to **God**.

—Italian proverb

"Never close your lips to those whom you have opened your heart."

—Charles Dickens

The quality of a **relationship** is a function of the extent to which it is built on a solid underlying friendship and meets the needs of the **two people involved**.

—Dr. Phil McGraw

"It doesn't matter if the guy is perfect or the girl is perfect, as long as they are perfect for each other."

—from the film *Good Will Hunting*
(Matt Damon and Ben Affleck, screenwriters)

'Tis better to have **loved** and **lost**
Than never to have loved at all.

—Alfred, Lord Tennyson

A **successful marriage** is an edifice
that must be rebuilt **every day.**

—André Maurois

Love sought is good, but given unsought, is better.

—Olivia, from *Twelfth Night*,

William Shakespeare

We cannot really love anybody with whom we never laugh.

—Agnes Repplier

"Love is like a flower: Once you pick it, it slowly dies."

—Anonymous

"If you want to sacrifice the admiration of many men for the criticism of one, go ahead, get married."

—Katharine Hepburn

You can rehearse a wedding but not a marriage.

—Al Batt

Never pretend to a love which you do not actually feel, for love is not ours to command.

—Alan Watts

"Once the realization
is accepted that even
between the closest
human beings infinite
distances continue, a
wonderful living side
by side can grow,
if they succeed in loving
the distance between
them which makes it
possible for each to see
the other whole against
the sky."

—Rainer Maria Rilke

I'm old-fashioned and a square. I believe people should not engage in sex too early. They will never forget that first sexual experience, and it would be a pity to just throw it away. So what's the rush? Hug and kiss and neck and pet, and **don't rush** into a sexual encounter.

—Dr. Ruth Westheimer

It is better to be looked over than overlooked.

—Mae West

"Do not let too strong a light come into your bedroom. There are in a beauty a great many things which are enhanced by being seen only in a half-light."

—Ovid

It doesn't make any difference what you do in the bedroom as long as you don't do it in the street and frighten the horses.

—Mrs. Patrick Campbell

I believe that love cannot be bought
except with love.

—John Steinbeck

Marriage has no guarantees.
If that's what you're looking for,
go live with a car battery.

—Erma Bombeck

Immature love says: "I love you because
I need you." Mature love says: "I need you
because I love you."

—Erich Fromm

"Love is everything
it's cracked up to be . . .
It really is worth fighting
for, being brave for,
risking everything for."

—Erica Jong

For women the best **aphrodisiacs**
are words. The G-spot is in the **ears**.
He who looks for it below there is
wasting his time.

—Isabel Allende

All married couples should learn
the art of battle as they should
learn the art of making love. Good
battle is objective and honest,
never vicious or cruel. Good battle
is healthy and constructive, and
brings to a marriage the principle
of equal partnership.

—Ann Landers

When angry, count ten before you
speak; if very angry, a hundred.

—Thomas Jefferson

"When angry, count to four; when very angry, swear."

—Mark Twain

While forbidden fruit is said to **taste sweeter,** it usually **spoils faster.**

—Abigail Van Buren ("Dear Abby")

Don't criticize in the sack. Discuss constructively later.

—Dr. Ruth Westheimer

If you think **marriage** is going to be perfect, you're probably **still** at your reception.

—Martha Bolton

"Remember, we all stumble, every one of us. That's why it's a comfort to go hand in hand."

—Emily Kimbrough

Friendship . . . is not something you learn in school. But if you haven't learned the meaning of friendship, you really **haven't learned anything.**

—Muhammad Ali

A true apology is more than just acknowledgment of a mistake. It is recognition that something you have said or done has damaged a relationship and that you care enough about the relationship to want it repaired and restored.

—Norman Vincent Peale

Grief can take care of itself, but to get the full value of a joy you must have somebody to divide it with.

—Mark Twain

If you can, help others; if you cannot do that, at least **do not harm them.**

—Tenzin Gyatso, 14th Dalai Lama

"Friendship is the only cement that will ever hold the world together."

—Woodrow Wilson

The most **important thing in life** is **giving back.**

—Michael R. Bloomberg

I'll tell you the same thing my mother used to tell me: "The most important thing in life is to try to do the very best for your neighbors. Respect other people."

—Hank Aaron

Be respectful to others as you grow . . . If we lack respect for one group, then there is a tendency for that attitude to spread. It becomes infectious and no one becomes safe from the ravages of prejudice.

—Walter Annenberg

Distrust all those who love you
extremely upon a very slight acquaintance
and without any visible reason.

—Lord Chesterfield

"Thy friend has a friend,
and thy friend's friend has
a friend; be discreet."

—The Talmud

Lots of people want to ride with you
in the limo, but what you want is someone
who will take the bus with you
when the limo breaks down.

—Oprah Winfrey

Every human being has value.
This is the basis of all healthy
relationships. Through living
each day as it is given to me,
I've learned that. It cannot be
"taught," but it can be "caught"
from those who live their lives
right along with us.

—Fred Rogers ("Mr. Rogers")

The real test of friendship is:
can you literally do nothing with the other
person? Can you enjoy those moments of
life that are **utterly simple?**

—Eugene Kennedy

Santa Claus has the **right idea.**
Visit people only **once a year.**

—Victor Borge

"Laughter is not at all a bad beginning for a friendship, and it is far the best ending for one."

—Oscar Wilde

Do not keep on with a mockery of friendship after the substance is gone— but part, while you **can part friends.** Bury the carcass of friendship: it is not worth embalming.

—William Hazlitt

Some people think only intellect counts: knowing how to solve problems, knowing how to get by, knowing how to identify an advantage and seize it. But the functions of intellect are insufficient without courage, love, friendship, compassion, and empathy.

—Dean Koontz

"All love that has not friendship for its base, is like a mansion built upon the sand."

—Ella Wheeler Wilcox

You shall judge a man by his foes as well as by his friends.

—Joseph Conrad

"It takes a long time to grow an old friend."

—John Leonard

It's the little things that matter, that add up in the end, with the priceless thrilling magic found only in a friend.

—Elizabeth Dunphy

The **first duty** of love is to **listen.**

—Paul Tillich

"Never assume, for it makes an ASS out of U and ME."

—Anonymous

Fish and visitors **stink** after three days.

—Benjamin Franklin

I tell you, the more I think, the more I feel that there is nothing more truly artistic than to love people.

—Vincent van Gogh

Hatred paralyzes life; love releases it. Hatred confuses life; love harmonizes it. Hatred darkens life; love illuminates it.

—Dr. Martin Luther King Jr.

Love doesn't just sit there, like a stone; it has to be made, like bread, remade all the time, made new.

—Ursula K. Le Guin

Love is not enough. It must be
the foundation, the cornerstone—
but not the complete structure.
It is much too pliable, too yielding.

—Bette Davis

Spread love everywhere you go.
Let no one ever come to you without
leaving happier.

—Mother Teresa

Never miss an opportunity to make
others happy, even if you have to
leave them alone in order to do it.

—Anonymous

"Always be nice to your children, because they are the ones who will choose your rest home."

—Phyllis Diller

Never raise your hand to your kids. It leaves your groin unprotected.

—Red Buttons

Always serve too much hot fudge sauce on hot fudge sundaes. It makes people **overjoyed,** and puts them in your debt.

—Judith Olney

"There is no remedy for love but to love more."

—Henry David Thoreau

It is not **self-sacrifice** to die protecting that which **you value:** If the value is great enough, you do not care to exist without it. This applies to any alleged sacrifice for **those one loves.**

—Ayn Rand

Love one another and you will be happy. It's as simple and as difficult as that.

—Michael Leunig

The truth is that there is only one terminal dignity—love. And the story of a love is not important—what is important is that one is capable of love. It is perhaps the only glimpse we are permitted of eternity.

—Helen Hayes

"You have to love your children unselfishly. That's hard. But it's the only way."

—Barbara Bush

If someone is too tired to give you a smile, leave one of your own, because no one needs a smile as much as those who have none to give.

—Rabbi Samson Hirsch

Love yourself first and everything else falls into line. You really have to love yourself to get anything done in this world.

—Lucille Ball

The most **important** thing a father can do for his children is to love their **mother**.

—Theodore M. Hesburgh

"The most important things to do in the world are to get something to eat, something to drink, and somebody to love you."

—Brendan Behan

A **total immersion** in life offers the best classroom for **learning to love.**

—Leo Buscaglia

If you wish to be loved, show more of your faults than your virtues.

—Edward Bulwer-Lytton

Until one has loved an animal, a part of one's soul **remains unawakened.**

—Anatole France

"There is only misfortune in not being loved; there is misery in not loving."

—Albert Camus

If you cannot **work with love** but only with distaste, it is better that you should **leave your work.**

—Kahlil Gibran

"Assist the reduced fellow man, either by a considerable gift or a sum of money or by teaching him a trade or by putting him in the way of business so that he may earn an honest livelihood and not be forced to the dreadful alternative of holding out his hand for charity. This is the highest step and summit of charity's golden ladder."

—Moses Maimonides

"If you have only one smile in you, give it to the people you love. Don't be surly at home, then go out in the street and start grinning 'Good morning' at total strangers."

—Maya Angelou

People are often unreasonable, illogical,
and self-centered;
Forgive them anyway.
If you are kind, people may accuse you
of selfish, ulterior motives;
Be kind anyway.
If you are successful, you will win some
false friends and some true enemies;
Succeed anyway.
If you are honest and frank, people may
cheat you;
Be honest and frank anyway.
What you spend years building,
someone could destroy overnight;
Build anyway.
If you find serenity and happiness,
they may be jealous;
Be happy anyway.

The good you do today, people will often
  forget tomorrow;
  Do good anyway.
Give the world the best you have, and it
  may never be enough;
  Give the world the best you have
  got anyway.
You see, in the final analysis, it is between
  you and God;
  It was never between you and
  them anyway.

—Mother Teresa

Chapter Six

Throw Your Dreams

{Advice to Inspire and Encourage}

Throw your dreams into space like a kite, and you do not know what it will bring back; a new life, a new friend, a new love, a new country.

—Anaïs Nin

Just don't give up trying to do what you really want to do. Where there is **love and inspiration,** I don't think you can go wrong.

—Ella Fitzgerald

If you can dream it, you can do it.

—Walt Disney

One of the things I learned the hard way was that it doesn't pay to get discouraged. Keeping busy and making optimism a way of life can restore your faith in yourself.

—Lucille Ball

Be yourself. The world worships the original.

—Ingrid Bergman

Be careful what you set your heart upon—for it will surely be yours.

—James Baldwin

What counts can't always be counted; what can be counted doesn't **always count.**

—Albert Einstein

The secret of life is in opening up your heart.

—Chita Rivera

You can **learn new things** at any time in your life if you're willing to be a beginner. If you actually learn to like being a beginner, the whole **world opens up to you.**

—Barbara Sher

"Don't be a blueprint.
Be an original."

—Roy Acuff

Most of the **important things in the world** have been accomplished by people who have kept on trying when there seemed to be **no hope at all.**

—Dale Carnegie

I slept and dreamt that life was joy. I awoke and saw that life was service. I acted and behold, service was joy.

—Rabindranath Tagore

Indulge your **imagination** in every
possible flight.

—Jane Austen

Only those who will risk going
too far can possibly find out how
far one can go.

—T. S. Eliot

Life is good only when it is magical and
musical, a perfect timing and consent, and
when we do not anatomise it. You must
treat the days respectfully . . . You must
hear the bird's song without attempting
to render it into nouns and verbs."

—Ralph Waldo Emerson

"A ship in port is safe, but that's not what ships are built for."

—Grace Hopper

Disappointment should be cremated, not embalmed.

—Henry S. Haskins

When one door closes, another opens; but we often look so long and so regretfully upon the closed door that we do not see the one which has opened for us.

—Helen Keller

"A man, as a general rule, owes very little to what he is born with—a man is what he makes of himself."

—Alexander Graham Bell

Shoot for the moon. Even if you miss, you'll land among the stars.

—Les Brown

Our **greatest glory** is not in never failing, but in rising up **every time we fail**.

—Ralph Waldo Emerson

Those who contemplate the **beauty of the earth** find reserves of strength that will endure **as long as life lasts.**

—Rachel Carson

"The most worthwhile thing is to try to put happiness into the lives of others."

—Sir Robert Baden-Powell

"Each time a man stands up for an ideal, or acts to improve the lot of others, or strikes out against injustice, he sends forth a tiny ripple of hope, and crossing each other from a million different centers of energy and daring, those ripples build a current that can sweep down the mightiest walls of oppression and resistance."

—Robert F. Kennedy

Resolve to **be thyself:** and know, that he
who finds himself, **loses his misery.**

—Matthew Arnold

Always remember that the
future comes one day at a time.

—Dean Acheson

For the past thirty-three years, I have looked
in the mirror every morning and
asked myself, "If today were the last day of
my life, would I want to do what I am about
to do today?" And whenever the answer
has been "No" for too many days in a row,
I know I need to **change something.**

—Steve Jobs

Quit now, you'll never make it.
If you disregard this advice, you'll
be **halfway there.**

—David Zucker

"There are only two
lasting legacies we can
hope to give our children.
One of these is roots;
the other, wings."

—Hodding Carter

We make a **living** by what we get,
but we **make a life** by what we give.

—Winston Churchill

The only true gift is a portion of yourself.

—Ralph Waldo Emerson

"Waste no more time arguing what a good man should be. Be one.

—Marcus Aurelius

Do something for somebody every day for which you do not get paid.

—Albert Schweitzer

Only a life lived in the service of others is worth living.

—Albert Einstein

"Remember always that you have not only the right to be an individual, you have an obligation to be one. You cannot make any useful contribution in life unless you do this."

—Eleanor Roosevelt

Thank God—every morning when you get up—that you have something to do which **must be done**, whether you like it or not. Being forced to work, and forced to do your best, will breed in you a hundred virtues which the idle will **never know**.

—Charles Kingsley

Be yourself.
Who else is better qualified?

—Frank J. Giblin II

Life consists not in holding good cards but in playing those you **hold well**.

—Josh Billings

Don't be afraid your life will end;
be afraid that it will never begin.

—Grace Hansen

Begin doing what you **want to do** now.
We are not living in eternity. We have only
this moment, **sparkling like a star** in
our hand—and melting like a snowflake.

—Sir Francis Bacon

The best remedy for those who are afraid,
lonely, or unhappy is to go outside, some-
where where they can be quiet, alone
with the heavens, **nature and God.**

—Anne Frank

Tranquility is like quicksilver. The harder
you grab for it, the less likely you will grasp it.

—Bern Williams

"Three grand essentials
to happiness in this life are
something to do, something
to love, and something to
hope for."

—Joseph Addison

To give **pleasure** to a single heart by a single kind act is better than a thousand head-bowings **in prayer.**

—Saadi

There are three ingredients to the good life;
learning, earning, and **yearning.**

—Christopher Morley

It is **difficult** to steer a parked car, so **get moving.**

—Henrietta Mears

Labor to keep alive in your breast that little spark of celestial fire called conscience.

—George Washington

There is a way to look **at the past.**
Don't hide from it. It will not catch you
if you **don't repeat it.**

—Pearl Bailey

"You must learn day by day,
year by year, to broaden
your horizon. The more
things you love, the more
you are interested in, the
more you enjoy, the more
you are indignant about,
the more you have left
when anything happens."

—Ethel Barrymore

Better keep yourself clean and bright; you are the window through which you must see the world.

—George Bernard Shaw

Seize the moment. Remember all those women on the *Titanic* who waved off the dessert cart.

—Erma Bombeck

To help yourself, help others. Whatever good you do travels a circle and returns to you many times over—but remember, life isn't about what you get, it's about what you become.

—Dennis Gaskill

"Look up and not down.
Look forward and not back.
Look out and not in, and
lend a hand."

—Edward Everett Hale

It is **folly for a man to pray** to the gods
for that which **he has the power** to
obtain by himself.

—Epicurus

Dwell not on the past. Use it to illustrate a point, then leave it behind. Nothing really matters except what you do now in this instant of time. From this moment onwards you can be an entirely different person, filled with love and understanding, ready with an outstretched hand, uplifted and positive in every thought and deed.

—Eileen Caddy

Your children **need your presence** more than your **presents**.

—Jesse Jackson

You must be the change you wish to see in the world.

—Mohandas Gandhi

Do, or do not. There is no "try."

—Yoda, *The Empire Strikes Back*
(screenplay by Leigh Brackett and
Lawrence Kasdan)

Everybody can be great . . . because anybody can serve. You don't have to have a college degree to serve. You don't have to make your subject and verb agree to serve. . . . You only need a heart full of grace. A soul generated by love.

—Dr. Martin Luther King Jr

"Whenever you feel the need or wish to cheer yourself, think about all of the good qualities of those around you—the energy of one, for instance, the modesty of another, the generosity of a third, and some other gift of a fourth. For nothing is ever so cheering as the images of the qualities shining through in the character of those who live with us. . . . Have these images then ever before your eyes."

—Marcus Aurelius

Treat a man as if he were what he ought to be and you help him become what he is capable of being.

—Johann von Goethe

Don't **compromise** yourself. You're **all you've got.**

—Janis Joplin

Carry out a random act of kindness, with no expectation of reward, safe in the knowledge that one day someone might do the same for you.

—Princess Diana

Do not look where **you fell,**
but where you **slipped.**

—Anonymous

"God, grant me the serenity
to accept the things I
cannot change; courage
to change the things I can;
and wisdom to know the
difference."

—Dr. Reinhold Niebuhr

(The Serenity Prayer)

If your **daily life** seems poor,
do not blame it; blame yourself,
tell yourself that you are not poet
enough to call forth **its riches.**

—Rainer Maria Rilke

Share and save the world.

—Maitreya

"**Act the way** you'd like to be
and soon you'll be the **way you act.**"

—George W. Crane

If you want a **quality,**
   act as if you **already had it.**
                                    —William James

Jack Kennedy always said to me,
   "Hedy, get involved. That's the
   secret of life. Try everything. Join
   everything. Meet everybody."
                                    —Hedy Lamarr

If you **really want something** in
   this life, you have to work for it. Now,
   quiet, they're about to announce the
   lottery numbers!
                          —Homer Simpson, *The Simpsons,*

                          Matt Groening

If you pray for a Cadillac
and God sends a jackass, ride it.

—Anonymous

Know yourself. Don't accept your dog's
admiration as **conclusive evidence**
that you are wonderful.

—Ann Landers

Be who you are and say what
you feel, because those who mind
don't matter, and those who
matter don't mind.

—Dr. Seuss (Theodor Geisel)

Don't wait for the last judgment—
it takes place every day.

—Albert Camus

Remember your humanity,
and forget the rest.

—Bertrand Russell

Look at a day when you are
supremely satisfied at the end.
It's not a day when you lounge
around doing nothing; it's
when you've had everything
to do, and you've done it.

—Lord Acton

"Finish each day and be done with it. You have done what you could; some blunders and absurdities have crept in; forget them as soon as you can. Tomorrow is a new day; you shall begin it serenely and with too high a spirit to be encumbered with your old nonsense."

—Ralph Waldo Emerson

You can't wait for **inspiration**. You have to **go after it** with a club.

—Jack London

Chapter Seven

Hit the Right Keys

{Advice on Creativity and the Arts}

There's **nothing remarkable** about it.
All one has to do is hit the right keys
at the right time and the **instrument**
plays itself.

—Johann Sebastian Bach

"When in doubt, make a
fool of yourself. There is a
microscopically thin line
between being brilliantly
creative and acting like the
most gigantic idiot on earth.
So what the hell, leap!"

—Cynthia Heimel

Creativity is allowing yourself to **make mistakes.** Art is knowing **which ones to keep.**

—Scott Adams

Curiosity is the key to creativity.

—Akio Morita

If you want to work on your **art,** work on your **life.**

—Anton Chekhov

Find a need and **fill it.**

—Ruth Stafford Peale

A long walk and grooming
with a well-mannered dog is
a Zen experience that leaves
you refreshed and in a
creative frame of mind.

—Dean Koontz

You can't depend on **your eyes**
when your imagination is **out of focus.**

—Mark Twain

Marry an **English major** and get a
good editor.

—Stephen Ambrose

"Iron rusts from disuse, stagnant water loses its purity, and in cold weather becomes frozen; even so does inaction sap the vigors of the mind."

—Leonardo da Vinci

When a thing **has been said,** and said well, have no scruple. Take it and copy it.

—Anatole France

A man's **style in any art** should be
like his dress—it should **attract as little
attention** as possible.

—Samuel Butler

Employ in everything a certain
casualness which conceals art and
creates the impression that what
is done and said is accomplished
without effort and without its
being thought about. It is from
this, in my opinion, that grace
largely derives.

—Baldassare Castiglione

Do not follow where the path may lead. Go instead where there is no path and **leave a trail.**

—Muriel Strode

"Anyone can make the simple complicated— creativity is making the complicated simple."

—Charles Mingus

Never judge a work of art by its **defects.**

—Washington Allston

Never pay attention to what critics say. Remember, a statue has **never** been set up in honor of a critic.

—Jean Sibelius

"Don't be an art critic, but paint; there lies salvation."

—Paul Cezanne

Art is the only thing you cannot punch a button for. You must do it the old-fashioned way. Stay up and really burn the midnight oil. **There are no compromises.**

—Leontyne Price

"To be truly creative,
you have to work beyond
what you know. Pushing
the envelope is what being
an artist is all about."

—John Ferrie

Take the best that exists and
make it better. If it doesn't exist,
create it.

—Sir Henry Royce

"Sometimes you've got
to let everything go—purge
yourself. If you are unhappy
with anything . . . whatever
is bringing you down,
get rid of it. Because you'll
find that when you're free,
your true creativity,
your true self comes out."

—Tina Turner

Technique alone is never enough.
You have to have **passion**. Technique
alone is just an embroidered pot holder.

—Raymond Chandler

Use what talents you possess:
the woods would be very silent
if no birds sang there except
those that sang best.

—Henry van Dyke

You should not give anybody the
power to decide what is **right
and wrong** in your creativity.

—Anaïs Nin

Creativity comes from trust.
Trust your instincts. And never
hope more than you work.

—Rita Mae Brown

Think left and think right and think
low and think high. Oh, the thinks
you can think up **if only you try!**

—Dr. Seuss (Theodor Geisel)

"Turn loose and have fun.
Give the audience a show."

—Roy Acuff

Whatever you do, kid, serve it **with**
a little dressing.

—George M. Cohan (to Spencer Tracy)

I believe entertainment can aspire to be art, and can become art, but if you set out to make art you're an idiot.

—Steve Martin

Show business is really 90 percent luck and 10 percent being able to handle it when it gets **offered to you**.

—Tommy Steele

If you've got talent, stick with it . . . because talent wins out, without a doubt.

—Bobby Sherman

Actors should be overheard, not listened to, and the audience is 50 percent of the performance.

—Shirley Booth

"'Get out of show business.' It's the best advice I ever got, because I'm so stubborn that if someone would tell me that, I would stay in it to the bitter end."

—Walter Matthau

"Here's my advice to you young comedians—live to be old comedians. I don't see how you can go wrong with that."

—George Burns

If you haven't struck oil in the first three minutes—stop boring.

—George Jessel

Chapter Eight

Imitate a Champion

{Advice on Sports and Competition}

The best and fastest way to
learn a sport is to watch and
imitate a champion.

—Jean-Claude Killy

Push yourself **again** and **again**.
Don't give an inch until the **final**
buzzer sounds.

—Larry Bird

The first thing is to love your sport.
Never do it to please someone
else. It has to be yours.

—Peggy Fleming

The race is not always to the swift, nor the battle to the strong, but that's **the way to bet.**

—Damon Runyon

"**Ask not what your teammates can do for you. Ask what you can do for your teammates.**"

—Earvin "Magic" Johnson

Warriors take chances. Like everyone else, they fear failing, but they **refuse to let fear** control them.

—Samurai proverb

The greatest efforts in sports
come when the mind is as still
as a glass lake.

—W. Timothy Gallwey

"Luck is the residue
of design."

—Branch Rickey

What you **lack in talent** can be
made up with desire, hustle, and
giving **110 percent all the time.**

—Don Zimmer

Loosen your girdle and let 'er fly!

—Babe Didrikson Zaharias

"Be bold. If you're going to make an error, make a doozy, and don't be afraid to hit the ball."

—Billie Jean King

It ain't over 'til it's over.

—Yogi Berra

An acre of performance is worth
a whole world of promise.

—Red Auerbach

Football **is like life**—it requires
perseverance, self-denial, hard work,
sacrifice, **dedication**, and respect
for authority.

—Vince Lombardi

Competitive sports are played
mainly on a five-and-a-half-inch
court—the space between your
ears.

—Bobby Jones

"And listen—you've got
to kid him. Get his goat.
Call him 'hot shot,' 'big
britches,' 'smarty pants,'
or even 'Toots,' until he
gets so nervous he doesn't
know which goal is which."

—A coach's advice to a rookie

football player, as quoted in a

1937 Wisconsin newspaper

Show me a guy who's **afraid to look
bad,** and I'll show you a guy **you can
beat every time.**

—Lou Brock

When you're riding, only the race in which you're riding **is important.**

—Bill Shoemaker

Talent wins games, but teamwork and intelligence win championships.

—Michael Jordan

The way a team plays as a whole determines its success. You may have the greatest bunch of individual stars in the world, but if they don't play together, the club won't be worth a dime.

—Babe Ruth

A champion is someone who
gets up when he can't.

—Jack Dempsey

Make the hard ones look easy
and the easy ones **look hard.**

—Walter Hagen

"Concentration is the
ability to think about
absolutely nothing
when it is absolutely
necessary."

—Ray Knight

How you **respond to the challenge** in the second half will determine what you become after the game, whether you are a **winner or a loser.**

—Lou Holtz

One hundred percent of shots not taken don't go in.

—Wayne Gretzky

I've always made a **total effort,** even when the odds seemed entirely against me. I never quit trying; **I never felt** that I didn't have **a chance to win.**

—Arnold Palmer

"My motto was always to keep swinging. Whether I was in a slump or feeling badly or having trouble off the field, the only thing to do was keep swinging."

—Hank Aaron

"Being number two sucks."

—Andre Agassi

You can **learn a line** from a win and a **book from a defeat.**

—Paul Brown

Defeat is worse than death because you have to live with defeat.

—Anonymous

You **can't win** unless you learn **how to lose.**

—Kareem Abdul-Jabbar

You gotta be careful with your body. Your body is like a bar of soap. The more you use it, the more it wears down.

—Richie Allen

It's not the size of the dog in the fight, but the size of the fight in the dog.

—Archie Griffin

"When you're playing for the national championship, it's not a matter of life or death. It's more important than that."

—Duffy Daugherty

The man who can drive himself further once the effort gets painful is the man who will win.

—Roger Bannister

You don't have the game you played last year or last week. **You only have today's game.** It may be far from your best, but that's all you've got. Harden your heart and **make the best of it.**

—Walter Hagen

You've got to get to the stage in life where going for it is more important than winning or losing.

—Arthur Ashe

There's only **one way** to become a hitter. Go up to the plate and get mad. **Get mad at yourself** and **mad at the pitcher.**

—Ted Willams

If you train hard, you'll not only
be hard, you'll be hard to beat.

—Herschel Walker

"I don't believe you have to
be better than everybody
else. I believe you have to
be better than you ever
thought you could be."

—Ken Venturi

Never break your putter and your driver
in the same round or **you're dead.**

—Golfer Tommy Bolt (known as
"terrible-tempered Tommy")

If everything's under control, you are going too slow.

—Mario Andretti

The key to any game is to use your strengths and hide your weaknesses.

—Paul Westphal

"When you lose, you're more motivated. When you win, you fail to see your mistakes and probably no one can tell you anything."

—Venus Williams

Chapter Nine

A Word to the Wise

{Proverbs and Other Folk Sayings}

A word to the wise **is sufficient.**

—Latin proverb

"To know the road ahead,
ask those coming back."

—Chinese proverb

If you're ridin' ahead of the herd,
take a look back every now and
then to make sure it's still there.

—Cowboy wisdom

A candle loses nothing by lighting another candle.

—Italian proverb

He who allows his day to pass by without practicing generosity and enjoying life's pleasures is like a blacksmith's bellows—he breathes but does not live.

—Sanskrit proverb

Write the bad things that are done to you in sand, but write the good things that happen to you on a piece of marble.

—Arabic saying

He who excuses himself, accuses himself.

—French proverb

Never miss a good chance to **shut up.**

—Cowboy wisdom

Lower your voice and strengthen your argument.

—Lebanese proverb

Words that soak into your ears
are whispered . . . not yelled.

—Cowboy wisdom

"Only your real friends will
tell you when your face is
dirty."

—Sicilian proverb

An ounce of patience is worth
a pound of brains.

—Dutch proverb

Time and Patience would
  bring the snail to Jerusalem.
                    —Irish proverb

"If you want to give
  God a good laugh,
  tell Him your plans."
                    —Yiddish proverb

Tell God the truth,
  but give the judge money.
                    —Russian proverb

He who wants a rose
must respect the thorn.

—Persian proverb

No matter **how far** you have gone
on the wrong road, **turn back.**

—Turkish proverb

Beginning is easy;
continuing is hard.

—Japanese proverb

Life is an echo; what you send out
comes back.

—Chinese proverb

When you give a lesson in
meanness to a critter or a
person, don't be surprised
if they learn their lesson.

—Cowboy wisdom

When you shoot an arrow of **truth**, dip its
point in **honey.**

—Arabian proverb

Even nectar is **poison** if taken in excess.

—Hindu proverb

"Grasp all, lose all."

—Italian proverb

If you want **happiness** for an **hour**,
take a nap.
If you want happiness for a **day,**
go fishing.
If you want happiness for a **year,**
inherit a fortune.
If you want happiness for a **lifetime,**
help somebody.

—Chinese proverb

When you are an anvil, be patient;
when a hammer, strike.

—Arabian proverb

How **beautiful** it is to do nothing,
and **then rest afterward.**

—Spanish proverb

Better a lean agreement than
a fat lawsuit.

—Yiddish proverb

Beware the person with nothing to **lose.**

—Italian proverb

"When you're throwin' your weight around, be ready to have it thrown around by somebody else."

—Cowboy wisdom

Deal with the **faults** of others as **gently as your own.**

—Chinese proverb

"Don't bet more than you can afford to lose."

—Spanish proverb

Who goes a-borrowing, goes a-sorrowing.

—English proverb

Better give a penny than lend twenty.

—Italian proverb

Giving alms never lessens
the purse.

—Spanish proverb

Better to go to bed hungry than to
wake up in debt.

—Russian proverb

"If you get a reputation
as an early riser,
you can sleep till noon."

—Irish proverb

If you want your dreams to come true, don't sleep.

—Yiddish proverb

"The quickest way to double your money is to fold it over and put it back in your pocket."

—Cowboy wisdom

When the fox preaches, take care of your geese.

—French proverb

If a man is as wise as a serpent,
he can afford to be as harmless
as a dove.

—Cheyenne proverb

Surrounding yourself with **dwarfs**
does not **make you a giant.**

—Yiddish proverb

If you get to thinkin' you're
a person of some influence,
try orderin' somebody else's
dog around.

—Cowboy wisdom

Don't be afraid to cry. It will free
your mind of sorrowful thoughts.

—Hopi saying

Ask about your neighbors,
then buy the house.

—Yiddish proverb

You'll never plow a field by
turning it over in your mind.

—Irish proverb

Life is simpler when you plow around
the stump.

—Cowboy wisdom

"Beware of still water, a still
dog, and a still enemy."

—Yiddish proverb

Always drink upstream from
the herd.

—Cowboy wisdom

Never rely on the glory of the morning
nor the smiles of your mother-in-law.

—Japanese proverb

"Don't judge a man by
the words of his mother;
listen to the comments
of his neighbors."

—Yiddish proverb

Fall seven times, **stand up** eight.

—Japanese proverb

If you find yourself in a hole,
the first thing to do is stop diggin'.

—Cowboy wisdom

"It's no use carrying an
umbrella if your shoes
are leaking."

—Irish proverb

When you meet a man, you judge
him by his clothes; when you
leave, you judge him by his heart.

—Russian proverb

When the **character of a man** is
not clear to you, **look at his friends.**

—Japanese proverb

"Confide a secret to a dumb
man and he will speak."

—Russian proverb

Remember that **silence** is sometimes
the best answer.

—Cowboy wisdom

Give neither counsel nor
salt till you are asked for it.

—Italian proverb

Lettin' the cat outta the bag is
a lot easier'n puttin' it back in!

—Cowboy wisdom

"Habits are at first cobwebs,
then cables."

—Spanish proverb

"Meanness don't jes'
happen overnight."

—Cowboy wisdom

If you chase two rabbits,
both will escape.

—Spanish proverb

"To run away is not
glorious, but very healthy."

—Russian proverb

Live a good, honorable life.
   Then when you get older and
   think back, you'll get to enjoy
   it a second time.

—Cowboy wisdom

If three people say you are an ass,
   put on a bridle.

—Spanish proverb

Never approach a bull from
   the front, a horse from the rear,
   or a fool from any direction.

—Cowboy wisdom

Do not tell the man carrying
you that he stinks.

—Sierra Leone proverb

Only a fool tests the depth of the water
with both feet.

—African proverb

Tell me and I'll forget. Show me,
and I may not remember. Involve
me, and I'll understand.

—Native American proverb

The best **sermons** are lived,
not preached.

—Cowboy wisdom

"Remember that your children are not your own, but are lent to you by the Creator."

—Mohawk proverb

He who would do **great things** should not attempt them **all alone.**

—Seneca proverb

Seek wisdom, not knowledge. Knowledge is of the past. Wisdom is of the future.

—Lumbee proverb

"Good judgment comes from experience. The problem is, a lot of experience comes from bad judgment."

—Cowboy wisdom

Avoid a friend who covers you with his wings and destroys you **with his beak.**

—Spanish proverb

"Cherish youth,
but trust old age."

—Pueblo proverb

Don't let **yesterday** use up too much
of **today.**

—Cherokee proverb

One is never too old to yearn.

—Italian proverb

Timing has a lot to do with the outcome of a **rain dance.**

—Cowboy wisdom

"Better is the smoke of one's own house than the fire of another's."

—Spanish proverb

Take only what you need and leave the land as you found it.

—Arapaho proverb

What goes **around**, comes **around**.

—Anonymous

With lies you may go ahead in the world, but you can never go back.

—Russian proverb

"Don't squat
with your spurs on."

—Cowboy wisdom

Chapter Ten

Enjoy Your Ice Cream

{Advice on Advice}

My advice to you is not to inquire why or whither, but just enjoy your ice cream while it's on your plate—that's my philosophy.

—Thornton Wilder

The true secret of giving advice is, after you have honestly given it, to be perfectly indifferent whether it is taken or not, and **never** persist in trying to set people right.

—Hannah Whitall Smith

"I always advise people never to give advice."

—P. G. Wodehouse

Seek ye counsel of the aged, for their eyes have looked on the faces of the years and their ears have hearkened to the voices of Life. Even if their counsel is displeasing to you, pay heed to them.

—Kahlil Gibran

When a man comes to me for advice, I find out the kind of advice he wants, and I give it to him.

—Josh Billings

All you **teenagers out there.** The big mistake you're making is that you listen to all that bad advice from kids your own age. You should listen to your parents. They're entitled to **give you bad advice.**

—George Burns

Write down the advice of him who loves you, though you like it not at present.

—Italian proverb

The **best advice I can give** is to ignore advice. Life is too short to be distracted by the **opinions of others.**

—Russell Edson

Best advice on writing I've ever received: Finish.

—Peter Mayle

"I have found the best way to give advice to your children is to find out what they want and then advise them to do it."

—Harry S. Truman

If it's free, it's advice; if you pay for it, **it's counseling;** if you can use either one, **it's a miracle.**

—Jack Adams

Advice is seldom welcome;
and those who want it the
most always like it the least.

—Lord Chesterfield

Advice would always be **more acceptable** if it **didn't conflict** with our plans.

—New England proverb

"Don't take a butcher's advice on how to cook meat. If he knew, he'd be a chef."

—Andy Rooney

"Ask advice only of your equals."

—Danish proverb

Never take the advice of someone who has not had your kind of trouble.

—Sidney J. Harris

In giving advice, **seek to help,** not please, your friend.

—Solon

People who ask our advice almost never take it. Yet we should never refuse to give it, upon request, for it often helps us to see our own way more clearly.

—Brendan Francis

The advice of friends must be received with a judicious reserve; we must not give ourselves up to it and follow it blindly, whether right or wrong.

—Pierre Charron

I owe my success to having listened respectfully to the very best advice, and then going away and doing the exact opposite.

—Gilbert K. Chesterton

The worst men often give the
best advice.

—Philip James Bailey

"To profit from good advice
requires more wisdom than
to give it."

—John Churton Collins

Give advice to learn from your own
hidden wisdom.

—Duane Alan Hahn

A good scare is worth more than good advice.

—Horace

No vice is so bad as advice.

—Marie Dressler

"When you encounter seemingly good advice that contradicts other seemingly good advice, ignore them both."

—Al Franken

Selected Quoted Sources

Aaron, Henry "Hank" (b. 1934), American baseball player
Abdul-Jabbar, Kareem (b. 1947), American basketball player
Acheson, Dean (1893–1971), U.S. Secretary of State
Acton, John Dalberg-Acton, Lord (1834–1902), British historian
Acuff, Roy (1903–1992), American country music singer
Adams, Jack (1895–1968), Canadian ice hockey player
Adams, Joey (1911–1999), American comedian
Adams, John (1735–1826), second U.S. president
Adams, John Quincy (1767–1848), sixth U.S. president
Adams, Scott (b. 1957), American cartoonist; creator of *Dilbert*
Addison, Joseph (1672–1719), British essayist
Aesop (620–560 BC), Greek fable author
Affleck, Ben (b. 1972), American actor
Agassi, Andre (b. 1970), American tennis player
Aiken, Howard (1900–1973), American pioneer in computer development
Alcott, Louisa May (1832–1888), American novelist
Alda, Alan (b. 1936), American actor and political activist
Algren, Nelson (1909–1981), American novelist
Ali, Muhammad (b. 1942), American prizefighter
Allen, Marcus (b. 1960), American football player
Allen, Richie (b. 1942), American baseball player
Allen, Woody (b. 1935), American comedian, actor, director, and producer
Allende, Isabelle (b. 1942), Chilean author
Allston, Washington (1779–1843), American poet and painter
Ambrose, Stephen (1936–2002), American historian
Andretti, Mario (b. 1940), American race car driver
Angelou, Maya (b. 1928), American poet, actress, and civil rights activist
Annenberg, Walter (1908–2002), American publisher and philanthropist
Aristophanes (448–380 BC), Greek dramatist

Aristotle (384–322 BC), Greek philosopher
Arnold, Matthew (1822–1888), British poet
Ash, Mary Kay (1918–2001), American businesswoman
Ashe, Arthur (1943–1993), American tennis player
Asimov, Isaac (1920–1992), American science fiction author
Astor, Nancy, Lady (1879–1964), British legislator and hostess
Auerbach, Arnold "Red" (b. 1917), American basketball coach
  and executive
Aurelius, Marcus (AD 121–180), Roman emperor and philosopher
Austen, Jane (1775–1817), British novelist
Bach, Johann Sebastian (1685–1750), German composer
Bacon, Sir Francis (1561–1626), British essayist and philosopher
Baden-Powell, Sir Robert (1857–1941), British founder of the Boy Scouts
Bailey, Pearl (1918–1990), American actress and singer
Bailey, Philip James (1816–1902), British poet
Baldwin, James (1924–1987), American author
Ball, Lucille (1911–1989), American actress
Banks, Ernie (b. 1931), American baseball player
Bannister, Roger (b. 1929), British track athlete; first man to run a
  four-minute mile
Barry, Dave (b. 1947), American humor columnist
Barrymore, Ethel (1879–1959), American actress
Beerbohm, Max (1872–1956), British author
Behan, Brendan (1923–1964), Irish playwright and short story author
Bell, Alexander Graham (1847–1922), Scottish scientist and inventor
Bellamy, Carol (b. 1942), American politician and UNICEF director
Bergman, Ingrid (1915–1982), Swedish actress
Berra, Lawrence "Yogi" (b. 1925), American baseball player
Billings, Josh (1818–1885), American humor essayist
Bird, Larry (b. 1956), American basketball player and coach
Blake, William (1757–1827), British poet
Bloomberg, Michael R. (b. 1942), American businessman and politician
Boetcker, William J. H., (1873–1962) American religious leader
Bolt, Tommy (b. 1918), American golfer
Bombeck, Erma (1927–1996), American author and columnist
Bonaparte, Napoleon (1769–1821), French emperor and general
Booth, Shirley (1898–1992), American actress

Borg, Bjorn (b. 1956), Swedish tennis player

Borge, Victor (1909–2000), Danish-American musical entertainer

Bose, Amar Gopal, (b. 1929), Indian American electrical engineer

Brackett, Leigh (1915–1978), American novelist and screenwriter

Brock, Lou (b. 1939), American baseball player

Brothers, Dr. Joyce (b. 1928), American psychologist and columnist

Brown, Les (b. 1945), American author and motivational speaker

Brown, Paul (1908–1991), American football coach

Brown, Rita Mae (b. 1944), American author and social activist

Buck, Pearl (1892–1973), American author

Buddha, Siddhartha Gautama (563–483 BC), Indian philosopher

Bulwer-Lytton, Edward (1803–1873), British novelist

Burns, George (1896–1996), American comedian and actor

Buscaglia, Leo (1924–1998), American psychology author

Bush, Barbara (b. 1925), U.S. First Lady; wife of President George H.
  Bush and mother of President George W. Bush

Butler, Samuel (1835–1902), British author

Buttons, Red (b. 1919), American comedian and actor

Campbell, Mrs. Patrick (1865–1940), British actress

Camus, Albert (1913–1960), French philosopher and author

Capone, Al (1899–1947), American racketeer

Carlyle, Thomas (1795–1881), British historian

Carnegie, Dale (1888–1955), American motivational speaker and author

Carson, Rachel (1907–1964), American ecologist and author

Carter, Hodding, III (b. 1935), American politician

Carver, George Washington (1864?–1943), American botanist

Carville, James (b. 1944), American political consultant and commentator

Castiglione, Baldassare (1478–1529), Italian author and diplomat

Castro, Fidel (b. 1926), premier of Cuba

Cezanne, Paul (1839–1906), French artist

Chandler, Raymond (1888–1959), American crime fiction author

Chanel, Coco (1883–1971), French fashion designer

Chaplin, Charles "Charlie" (1889–1977), British comic actor

Charron, Pierre (1541–1603), French philosopher

Chekhov, Anton (1860–1904), Russian author

Chesterfield, Philip Stanhope, Earl of (1694–1773), British statesman
  and author

Chesterton, Gilbert K. (1874–1936), British author
Child, Julia (1912–2004), American chef and author
Christie, Agatha (1890–1976), British crime fiction author
Churchill, Sir Winston (1874–1965), British statesman and author
Cleese, John (b. 1939), British comedian and actor
Clemens, Samuel; *See* Mark Twain
Clooney, George (b. 1961), American actor
Cohan, George M. (1878–1942), American songwriter, playwright, and
    entertainer
Collins, John Churton (1848–1908), British literary critic
Confucius (551–479 BC), Chinese philosopher and reformer
Conrad, Joseph (1857–1924), Polish-British novelist
Cousins, Norman (1915–1990), American magazine editor and essayist
Currie, Edwina (1946), British member of Parliament
Dali, Salvador (1904–1989), Spanish painter
Damon, Matt (b.1970), American film actor
Daugherty, Duffy (1915–1987), American football coach
da Vinci, Leonardo (1452–1519), Italian artist, inventor, and engineer
Davis, Bette (1908–1989), American film actress
de Montaigne, Michel (1533–1592), French essayist and humanist
Dempsey, Jack (1895–1983), American prizefighter
Diana, Princess of Wales (1961–1997), British celebrity royal
Dickens, Charles (1812–1870), British novelist
Diller, Phyllis (b. 1917), American comedian
Disney, Walt (1901–1966), American film animator and producer
Dressler, Marie (1868–1934), Canadian actress
Drucker, Peter F. (1909–2005), American business author and economist
Edelman, Marian Wright (b. 1939), American lawyer and civil rights
    advocate
Edison, Thomas (1847–1931), American inventor and businessman
Edson, Russell (b. 1935), American poet
Einstein, Albert (1879–1955), German physicist
Eisenhower, Dwight D. (1890–1969), thirty-fourth U.S. president
Eliot, T. S. (1888–1965), American-British playwright, poet, and essayist
Elizabeth II (b. 1926), British monarch
Emerson, Ralph Waldo (1803–1882), American philosopher and poet
Epictetus (AD 55–135), Greek philosopher

Epicurus (341–270 BC), Greek philosopher

Feinstein, Dianne (b. 1933), U.S. senator

Ferber, Edna (1885–1968), American novelist and screenwriter

Fields, W. C. (1880–1946), American comic actor

Fisher, Dorothy Canfield (1879–1958), American author

Fitzgerald, Ella (1917–1996), American jazz singer

Fleming, Peggy (b. 1948), American figure skater

Fonteyn, Margot (1919–1991), British ballet dancer

Forbes, Malcolm (1919–1990), American magazine publisher

Ford, Henry (1863–1947), American industrialist

France, Anatole (1844–1924), French novelist and short story author

Francis of Assisi, Saint (1182–1226), Italian cleric and patron saint of animals

Frank, Anne (1929–1945), German diarist

Franken, Al (b. 1951), American humorist, author, and radio personality

Franklin, Benjamin (1706–1790), American statesman and author

Fromm, Erich (1900–1980), German psychologist and philosopher

Frost, Robert (1874–1963), American poet

Fuller, Margaret (1810–1850), American journalist and women's rights activist

Gandhi, Indira (1917–1984), Indian stateswoman

Gandhi, Mohandas (1869–1948), Indian political and spiritual leader

Gates, Bill (b. 1955), American computer software entrepreneur

Gibbons, James Cardinal (1834–1921), Roman Catholic Archbishop of Baltimore

Gibran, Kahlil (1883–1931), Lebanese poet and artist

Goldwyn, Samuel (1882–1974), American movie producer

Greeley, Horace (1811–1872), American newspaper editor

Green, Celia (b. 1935), British intellectual and author

Gretzky, Wayne (b. 1961), Canadian ice hockey player and coach

Griffin, Archie (b. 1954), American football player

Groening, Matt (b.1954), American cartoonist, creator of *The Simpsons* television series

Hackett, Buddy (1924–2003), American comedian and actor

Hagen, Walter (1892–1969), American golfer

Hale, Edward Everett (1822–1909), American clergyman and author

Hayes, Helen (1900–1993), American actress

Hazlitt, William (1778–1830), British critic and essayist
Hein, Piet (1905–1996), Danish scientist and poet
Hemingway, Ernest (1899–1961), American author
Hepburn, Katharine (1907–2003), American stage and film actress
Hesburgh, Theodore M., Father (b. 1917), American cleric and academic
Hirsch, Samson (1808–1888), German rabbi
Holtz, Lou (b. 1937), American football coach
Hopper, Grace (1906–1992), American naval officer and computer developer
Horace (65–8 BC), Roman poet
Hubbard, Elbert (1856–1915), American author
Hubbard, Kin [Frank McKinney] (1868–1930), American cartoonist, humorist, and journalist
Hughes, Charles Evans (1862–1948), Chief Justice of U.S. Supreme Court
Huxley, Aldous (1894–1963), British author
Huxley, Thomas Henry (1825–1895), British biologist and philosopher
Ibsen, Henrik (1828–1906), Norwegian dramatist
Jackson, Jesse (b. 1941), American civil rights leader and politician
James, William (1842–1910), American philosopher
Jefferson, Thomas (1743–1826), third U.S. president
Jessell, George (1898–1981), American comedian
Jobs, Steven (b. 1955), American computer entrepreneur
Johnson, Earvin "Magic" (b. 1959), American basketball player
Johnson, Samuel (1709–1784), British author
Jones, Bobby (1902–1971), American golfer
Jong, Erica (b. 1942), American author
Joplin, Janis (1943–1970), American pop singer
Jordan, Michael (b. 1963), American basketball player
Kafka, Franz (1883–1924), Czech author
Kasdan, Lawrence (b. 1949), American screenwriter and producer
Kaufman, George S. (1889–1961), American playwright, director, and journalist
Kaufman, Margo (1954–2000), American columnist
Keller, Helen (1880–1968), American author, activist, and lecturer
Kennedy, Florynce (b. 1916), American civil rights leader
Kennedy, John Fitzgerald (1917–1963), thirty-fifth U.S. president
Kennedy, Robert F. (1925–1968), U.S. senator and attorney general

Killy, Jean-Claude (b. 1943), French skier

Kimbrough, Emily (1899–1989), American author and editor

King, Billie Jean (b. 1943), American tennis player

King Jr., Martin Luther (1929–1968), American minister and civil rights activist

Kingsley, Charles (1819–1875), British novelist and clergyman

Knight, Ray (b. 1952), American baseball player

Koontz, Dean (b. 1945), American novelist

Lamarr, Hedy (1914–2000), Austrian-American actress and inventor

Landers, Ann [Esther Lederer] (1918–2002), American newspaper advice columnist

Lao-tzu (4th century BC), Chinese Taoist philosopher

Le Guin, Ursula K. (b. 1929), American author

Lehman, Herbert (1878–1963), American politician

Leunig, Michael (b. 1945), Australian political cartoonist

Levenson, Sam (1911–1980), American humorist

Lichtenberg, Georg C. (1742–1799), German physicist and author

Lombardi, Vince (1913–1970), American football coach

London, Jack (1876–1916), American author

Longfellow, Henry Wadsworth (1807–1882), American poet

Lorimer, George Horace (1868–1937), American magazine editor

Mahfouz, Naguib (b. 1911), Egyptian novelist

Maimonides, Moses (1135–1204), Spanish-Jewish philosopher and physician

Maitreya (b. 1944), Persian religious leader

Marshall, George C. (1880–1959), American general and statesman

Martin, Judith [Miss Manners] (b. 1938), American etiquette expert

Martin, Steve (b. 1945), American comedian, writer, producer, and actor

Matthau, Walter (1920–2000), American actor

Maugham, W. Somerset (1874–1965), British novelist, playwright, and short story author

Maurois, André (1885–1967), French author

Mayle, Peter (b. 1939), British author

McGraw, Dr. Phil (b. 1950), American television personality

Mencken, Henry L[ouis] (1880–1956), American editor and critic

Menninger, William C. (1899–1966), American physician and entrepreneur

Mingus, Charles (1922–1979), American jazz musician

Mitchell, Maria (1818–1889), American astronomer
Mizner, Wilson (1876–1933), American screenwriter
Molière, Jean-Baptiste (1622–1673), French dramatist
Montessori, Maria (1870–1952), Italian educator and physician
Morley, Christopher (1890–1957), American poet, novelist, and journalist
Morita, Akio (1921–1999), Japanese businessman
Munro, H[ector] **H**[ugh] [pen name Saki] (1870–1916), British author
Nash, Ogden (1902–1971), American poet
Niebuhr, Dr. Reinhold (1892–1971), German theologian
Nin, Anaïs (1903–1977), French-American author
Nixon, Richard (1913–1994), thirty-seventh U.S. president
Onassis, Aristotle (1900–1975), Greek businessman
Osmond, Marie (b. 1959), American entertainer
Ovid (43 BC–AD 17), Roman poet
Paige, Leroy "Satchel" (1906–1982), American baseball player
Palmer, Arnold (b. 1929), American golfer
Patton, George S. (1885–1945), U.S. Army general in World War II
Peale, Norman Vincent (1898–1993), American minister and author
Peale, Ruth Stafford (b. 1906), American religious author and speaker
Penney, J. C. (1875–1971), American businessman and entrepreneur
Peters, Tom (b. 1942), American business management guru
Plato (427–347 BC), Greek philosopher
Pope, Alexander (1688–1744), British poet and satirist
Post, Emily (1873–1960), American etiquette authority
Price, Leontyne (b. 1927), American opera singer
Prudden, Bonnie (b. 1914), American rock climber
Rand, Ayn (1905–1982), Russian-American philosopher and author
Raymond, Eric S. (b. 1957), American author
Repplier, Agnes (1858–1950), American essayist
Richards, Keith (b. 1943), British rock musician
Rickey, Branch (1881–1965), American baseball executive
Rilke, Rainer Maria (1875–1926), Austrian author
Rivera, Chita (b. 1933), American actress and dancer
Robbins, Anthony (b. 1960), American motivational speaker and author
Rogers, Fred [Mr. Rogers] (1928–2003), American television
  personality
Rogers, Will (1879–1935), American humorist and performer

Rohn, Jim (b. 1931), American motivational speaker and author
Rooney, Andy (b. 1919), American columnist and television commentator
Roosevelt, Eleanor (1884–1962), U.S. First Lady and diplomat
Roosevelt, Theodore (1858–1919), twenty-sixth U.S. president
Royce, Henry (1863–1933), British pioneering car manufacturer
Runyon, Damon (1884–1946), American author and journalist
Ruskin, John (1819–1900), British author, artist, and poet
Russell, Bertrand (1872–1970), British logician, philosopher, and mathematician
Ruth, George Herman "Babe" (1895–1948), American baseball player
Saadi (1184–1283/1291?), Persian poet
Saki; *See* H. H. Munro
Santayana, George (1863–1952), Spanish philosopher, essayist, poet, and novelist
Schulz, Charles (1922–2000), American cartoonist; creator of *Peanuts*
Schweitzer, Albert (1875–1965), German physician, musician, and theologian
Seneca, Lucius Annaeus (4 BC–AD 65), Roman philosopher, statesman, and dramatist
Seuss, Dr. [pseudonym of Theodore Seuss Geisel] (1904–1991), American children's books author and illustrator
Shakespeare, William (1564–1616), British dramatist
Shaw, George Bernard (1856–1950), Irish dramatist and critic
Shaw, Henry Wheeler; *See* Josh Billings
Sherman, Bobby (b.1943), American pop singer and actor
Shoemaker, Bill (1931–2003), American jockey
Sibelius, Jean (1865–1957), Finnish composer
Smith, Hannah Whitall (1832–1911), American Christian mystic and suffragette
Smith, Liz (b. 1923), American author and journalist
Smith, Logan Pearsall (1865–1946), American essayist
Smith, Sydney (1771–1845), British author and clergyman
Socrates (ca. 470–399 BC), Greek philosopher
Solon (c. 638–558 BC), Greek statesman and poet
Steele, Tommy (b. 1936), British pop singer
Steinbeck, John (1902–1968), American novelist and screenwriter

Stewart, Jon (b. 1962), American television personality
Swanson, Claude (1862–1939), American lawyer and politician
Swift, Jonathan (1667–1745), British author and satirist
Tagore, Rabindranath (1861–1941), Indian poet, philosopher, author, and dramatist
Tennyson, Alfred, Lord (1809–1892), British poet
Tenzin, Gyatso (b. 1935), Tibetan fourteenth Dalai Lama
Teresa, Mother (1910–1997), Albanian-Indian nun and social activist
Thoreau, Henry David (1817–1862), American author, naturalist, and philosopher
Thurber, James (1894–1961), American humorist
Tillich, Paul (1886–1965), German theologian and philosopher
Todd, Mike (1907 or 1909–1958), American movie producer
Truman, Harry S. (1884–1972), thirty-third U.S. president
Trump, Donald (b. 1946), American real estate entrepreneur
Tse-tung, Mao (1893–1976), Chinese leader
Turner, Tina (b. 1939), American pop singer
Twain, Mark [pen name of Samuel L. Clemens] (1835–1910), American humorist and author
Van Buren, Abigail [pseudonym of Pauline and Jeanne Phillips], American newspaper advice columnists
Vanderbilt, Amy (1908–1974), American authority on etiquette
van Dyke, Henry (1852–1933), American clergyman, educator, and author
van Gogh, Vincent (1853–1890), Dutch painter
Venturi, Ken (b. 1931), American golfer
von Ebner-Eschenbach, Marie (1830–1916), Austrian author
von Goethe, Johann Wolfgang (1749–1832), German novelist, scientist, and philosopher
Walker, Herschel (b. 1962), American football player
Washington, George (1732–1799), first U.S. president
Watts, Alan (1915–1973), British author and philosopher
Welch, Jack (b.1935), American businessman
West, Jessamyn (1902–1984), American author
West, Mae (1892?–1980), American actress
Westheimer, Dr. Ruth (b. 1928), American author and therapist
Westphal, Paul (b. 1950), American basketball player and coach
Wilcox, Ella Wheeler (1850–1919), American author and poet

Wilde, Oscar (1854–1900), Irish dramatist

Wilder, Thornton (1897–1975), American novelist and playwright

Williams, Ted (1918–2002), American baseball player

Williams, Venus (b. 1980), American tennis player

Wilson, Woodrow (1856–1924), twenty-eighth U.S. president

Winfrey, Oprah (b. 1954), American television personality, actress, and producer

Wodehouse, P. G. (1881–1975), British novelist and short story author

Woolf, Virginia (1882–1941), British author and feminist

Youngman, Henny (1906–1998), American comedian

Zaharias, Mildred "Babe" Didrikson (1911–1956), American athlete

Zanuck, Darryl (1902–1979), American movie producer

Zapata, Emiliano (1879–1919), Mexican revolutionary

Zeta-Jones, Catherine (b. 1969), Welsh actress

Zimmer, Don (b. 1931), American baseball player and manager

Zucker, David (b. 1947), American movie director